FUELLING THE BODY

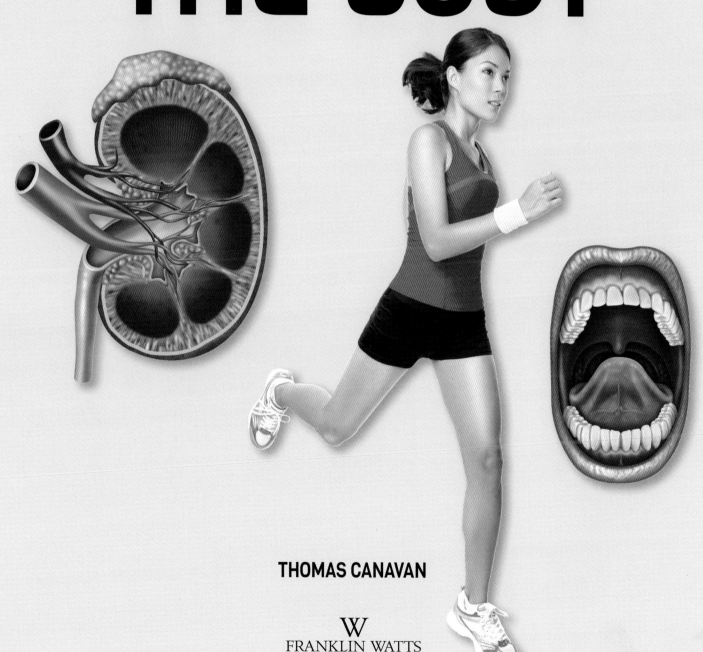

THOMAS CANAVAN

W
FRANKLIN WATTS
LONDON · SYDNEY

First published in 2015 by Franklin Watts

Copyright © Arcturus Holdings Limited

Franklin Watts
338 Euston Road
London NW1 3BH

Franklin Watts Australia
Level 17/207 Kent Street, Sydney NSW 2000

Produced by Arcturus Publishing Limited,
26/27 Bickels Yard, 151–153 Bermondsey Street, London SE1 3HA

Author: Thomas Canavan
Editors: Joe Harris, Joe Fullman, Nicola Barber and Sam Williams
Designer: Elaine Wilkinson
Original design concept and cover design: Notion Design

Picture Credits:
All images courtesy of Shutterstock, apart from: iStock.com: p9 bottom-right. Science Photo Library: p18 (Dorling Kindersley). Lee Montgomery and Anne Sharp: back cover, p30, p31.

A CIP catalogue for this book is available from the British Library.

Dewey Decimal Classification Number: 612.3

ISBN: 978 1 4451 4336 1

Printed in China

Franklin Watts is a division of Hachette Children's Books, an Hachette UK company.
www.hachette.co.uk

SL004509UK

Supplier: 13, Date 0315, Print run 3891

CONTENTS

FUELLING THE
BODY.

Your body has to break down the food you eat in order to get their nutrients, which are the substances you need to keep healthy. This process is called digestion, and it begins the moment food enters your mouth. For your food, this is the start of a long journey. Along the way, your digestive system churns, pushes, squeezes and breaks down the food until all of the nutrients are released into your body.

The process of digestion usually takes hours, although your body can process some foods and drinks more quickly. Your digestive system has many tools to get the job done efficiently – powerful chemicals, strong acids, expanding organs and muscles that work continuously without you even realizing it!

OPEN WIDE

Which food do you like best? Is it ice cream or a juicy peach, chips or a delicious pizza? Is your mouth watering even as you think about it? When your mouth starts to produce saliva (or spit) at the idea of something tasty, it's really getting ready to go to work!

Incisors

Upper lip

Molars

FIRST STOP

First, your teeth cut and grind up your food. Depending on their shape and where they are in your mouth, your teeth do different jobs. Sharp, narrow teeth called incisors at the front of your mouth cut food into small bits. The wider molars towards the back of your mouth grind up these pieces of food. Your tongue stands guard, keeping the food near to your teeth until it's been fully chewed.

Tongue

Sublingual glands

Canines

Lower lip

If you have jelly for dessert, set a bowl aside. Mix in some pineapple or kiwi fruit and leave for ten minutes. You'll see that the gelatin has become liquid. That's because these fruits contain a chemical that breaks the gelatin down – just as your saliva breaks down the food in your mouth.

JUICY!

Saliva moistens your food and helps to make it mushy. It also helps to break down food that may be trapped between your teeth – so it helps prevent tooth decay as well. A nice smell, such as freshly baked bread, can sometimes 'make your mouth water'. That's because your senses of smell and taste are very closely linked.

SOAKING IT ALL UP

Saliva is made by glands in your mouth. These are the sublingual glands, which lie below the tongue, and the parotid glands at the back of your mouth. Food needs to be moist before it can be digested. Saliva does that job. It's made of water and other chemicals. One of those chemicals is called amylase, which starts to break down your food even before you swallow.

Parotid glands

Sublingual glands

EASY TO SWALLOW

Once your food has been chewed and softened with saliva, your tongue rolls it into a ball, called a bolus. Then your tongue pushes this mushed-up bolus to the back of your mouth ready for the next stage in your food's digestive journey.

Your mouth contains more bacteria than the combined populations of the United States and Canada.

DOWN THE HATCH

You've chewed that tasty morsel and your tongue has rolled it into a ball. Now it's time to send it on its way to your stomach. But as it heads down your throat, there's a fork in the road: will it go straight to your stomach or wind up stuck in your windpipe?

Nose

Pharynx

Mouth

Trachea (windpipe)

SIDE BY SIDE

The pharynx is the area at the back of your mouth that leads into your throat. It deals with both eating and breathing. Your food passes that way, as well as the air being breathed in through your nose. Your food heads down your gullet, to your stomach. Meanwhile, air passes through your trachea (windpipe) to your lungs. The openings to these two passageways are right next door to each other.

GONE THE WRONG WAY?

If you drink too quickly you may start to cough. That's because some of the liquid went down 'the wrong way'. When you swallow, a flap called the epiglottis stops liquid and food from entering your trachea. If your epiglottis doesn't close in time, some of the drink may go into your trachea. You automatically cough to send the liquid straight back out, so you don't choke!

SAFE SWALLOWING

You can't eat and breathe at the same time – it would mean keeping both your trachea and gullet open at the same time. And that would be a recipe for disaster! You'd choke because the food would block your breathing. But a clever bit of design means that just as you are about to swallow, your epiglottis folds down to cover the top of your trachea. So when you swallow, your food heads safely down your gullet.

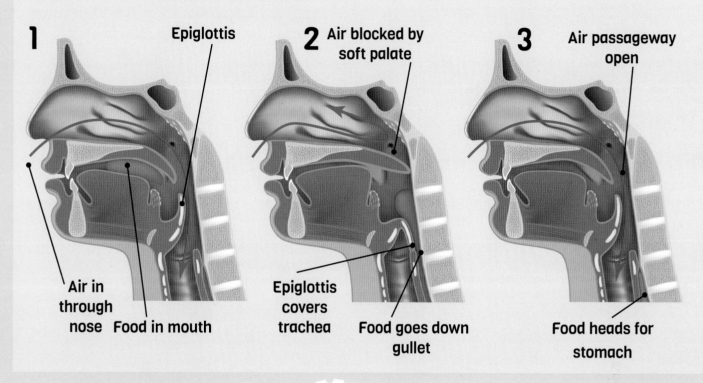

1 Epiglottis

Air in through nose — Food in mouth

2 Air blocked by soft palate

Epiglottis covers trachea — Food goes down gullet

3 Air passageway open

Food heads for stomach

Burping is the way your body gets rid of air that you accidentally swallowed. In some countries, letting out a soft burp is a sign that you've enjoyed your food!

FEELING THE SQUEEZE

Food doesn't just drop down your gullet. Circular muscles around your gullet tighten behind the bolus of food and remain relaxed in front of it. This makes it easier for it to slide down. The process is called peristalsis. It's a bit like eating a frozen ice lolly – you squeeze behind the ice to push it out the open end.

STOMACH CHURNING

Your food takes no more than ten seconds to pass through into your stomach. That's where the real process of digestion starts to happen. Your stomach is shaped like a letter J. It is one of the most important organs in your digestive system. A stomach is normally about the size of your fist, but it stretches and gets bigger as you fill it up with food.

GETTING TO WORK

All the work of mashing and churning the food happens in the body of your stomach. This is where those balls of food that come down your gullet get turned into a mushy liquid. The powerful muscles in the walls of your stomach squeeze the food. At the same time, the stomach wall produces enzymes and strong acids called gastric juices to break down the food further. After some squeezing and dissolving, the food turns into a liquid called chyme.

Gullet

Cardiac sphincter

Pylorus sphincter

Pyloric

Body of stomach

To small intestine

Powerful muscles

Gullet

Stomach

ONE-WAY SYSTEM

Your stomach is just one part of a whole series of different organs through which food passes as it's digested. Before entering the stomach, food travels down the gullet, and after leaving the stomach, it travels into the small intestine at the other end. Special valves called sphincters control the flow of food at each end. They make sure that food travels the right way through your body.

The acid in your stomach is strong enough to dissolve metal – but it wouldn't be a very tasty meal!

BELLY BALLOON

Your stomach expands just like a balloon as it fills with digested food.

BURNING UP

Sometimes, food and gastric juice from the stomach goes the wrong way through a sphincter, back into the gullet. Stomach acid in the base of the gullet causes heartburn – which can be very painful.

UNDER CONTROL

Special cells in your stomach wall (shown left) allow it to expand. They also control the balance of chemicals – so your stomach doesn't start to digest itself!

BIG AND SMALL

All that chewing, mushing and acid treatment gets your food good and squishy by the time it leaves your stomach. It's now ready for the next stage of digestion – removing the nutrients and getting rid of what's not needed. And this is when the small and large intestines have their starring roles.

NOT SO SMALL!

Your mushed-up food leaves the stomach and enters the small intestine. The small intestine isn't really small – it's just narrower than the large intestine. The food spends around four hours working its way through the sections of this intestine. In the first bit – the duodenum – it gets broken down even further. In the second and third bits, nutrients and vitamins are absorbed into your body's bloodstream.

The small intestine is much longer than the large intestine! Uncoiled, it would stretch 6 m (20 ft). That's more than the height of three basketball players standing on each other's shoulders!

Stomach

Transverse colon

Large intestine

Ascending colon

Descending colon

Small intestine

Rectum

Anus

FINGER FOOD

The lining of the small intestine is covered with tiny, narrow shapes called villi (and even tinier microvilli). Through a powerful microscope, villi look like tiny fingers swaying gently as they stir up your food. Villi are very good at removing nutrients and passing them to the blood that's heading to the rest of your body. Some of the villi are only two cells thick – so nutrients can pass through them easily.

LAST CHANCE

The large intestine is your body's last chance to extract nutrients from what you ate hours before. But there's more going on than simply getting the last bits of goodness from the food mixture. Many different types of bacteria live in the large intestine. Some of them produce important vitamins and chemicals. These get absorbed into your bloodstream along with everything else.

EVERY LAST DROP

The large intestine is much shorter than the small intestine, but it's called 'large' because it's wider. By the time your food moves into the large intestine, most of the important nutrients have been absorbed, but there's still some more to be collected – along with water. The food mixture (now mostly waste) is pretty dry when it moves through the descending colon into the rectum. And there it stays until you go to the toilet.

OUT YOU GO!

The rectum is the end of the line as far as your digestive system is concerned. It's like a storage room for waste – waiting there until you go to the toilet. And when you do, the waste is pushed out through peristalsis, the same way the food was pushed down your gullet. Sphincter muscles keep your anus – the real end of the line – tightly shut until you decide that you're ready to use the lavatory.

A BALANCED DIET

It's important to eat a healthy, balanced diet to give your body the wide range of nutrients it needs. It's fine to eat pizza or ice cream from time to time – as long as you eat lots of other healthy foods too!

IT'S GOOD FOR YOU!

The saying 'you are what you eat' is surprisingly true. The minerals, vitamins and other nutrients in your food are absorbed into your body, becoming part of it. Some help specific parts of your body, such as calcium in milk, which is excellent for building bones and teeth. Others help your whole body. Carbohydrates in pasta and rice give your body energy and keep you moving.

WHAT YOUR BODY NEEDS:

BRAIN - You need magnesium (from leafy vegetables) and vitamin E (present in many nuts) to help the brain to function well.

MUSCLES - Protein (in meat, fish, nuts and beans) helps build muscles.

BONES - Calcium (in most dairy products) keeps bones strong.

HAIR - Iron, vitamins A and C, protein and zinc (from a range of foods) keep your hair strong and shiny.

HEART - Your heart is a muscle, so it has all of the requirements of a normal muscle.

SKIN - Vitamin E (in avocados and pine nuts) and the chemicals in many fruits help your skin.

FINGERNAILS - Zinc, protein and some fatty acids (from oily fish) all keep your nails looking good.

BRAIN FOOD?

For centuries, fish was known as 'brain food'. Was that just a myth? Scientists now agree that some fatty acids really do help the brain. And the food that contains these acids – actually it's fish!

SUPERFOODS?

Some people describe blueberries, pomegranate juice, garlic, broccoli and other foods as 'superfoods'. They claim that these foods and drinks can help fight disease, keep you healthy and even help you live longer. Scientists agree that while all these foods are good for you, they don't work miracles! Far more important is to eat a 'super diet' – the balanced diet that gives your body the wide range of nutrients it needs to work well.

NAUGHTY BUT NICE!

Foods such as ice cream and pizza should be occasional treats. Most ice cream contains lots of fat and sugar, and pizza is heavy in fat. Although your body needs some fat in a balanced diet, it doesn't require a lot, and too much of the types of fats found in foods like sausages, cheese or cookies can cause health problems.

Your body contains enough iron to make a spike large enough to hold your weight!

HELPFUL ALLIES

Many of your body's digestive organs are found close to each other in your abdomen. That's the part of your body that's just above and below your belly button. The liver, pancreas and gall bladder all play their part in helping you digest food.

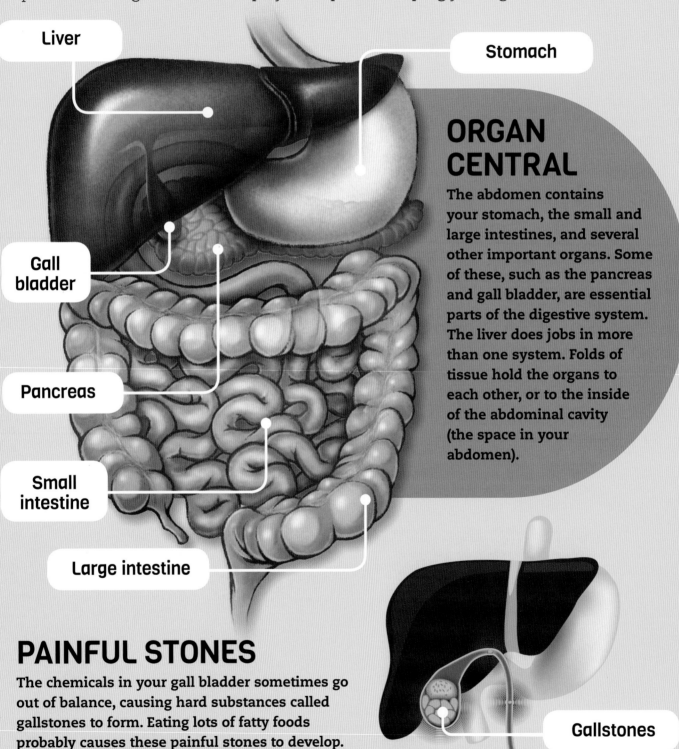

Liver

Stomach

Gall bladder

Pancreas

Small intestine

Large intestine

ORGAN CENTRAL

The abdomen contains your stomach, the small and large intestines, and several other important organs. Some of these, such as the pancreas and gall bladder, are essential parts of the digestive system. The liver does jobs in more than one system. Folds of tissue hold the organs to each other, or to the inside of the abdominal cavity (the space in your abdomen).

PAINFUL STONES

The chemicals in your gall bladder sometimes go out of balance, causing hard substances called gallstones to form. Eating lots of fatty foods probably causes these painful stones to develop.

Gallstones

INTO THE MIX

The pancreas makes substances called enzymes. These are used in your small intestine to break down carbohydrates, proteins and fats. It also makes and sends a chemical called bicarbonate of soda to the small intestine. The bicarbonate of soda reacts with the acid in the intestine, stopping it from getting too strong and damaging the lining of the small intestine.

ACTIVITY

Put three teaspoons of bicarbonate of soda into an empty plastic bottle. Pour in a cup of vinegar and stretch a balloon across the top of the bottle. Soon, the balloon fills up. That's because the bicarbonate and vinegar (acid) react – just as bicarbonate and acid juices do in the intestine.

STAR PLAYER

If you were asked to name your most important organ, you would probably say your heart (pictured on the right). But after looking at the liver closely, you might think twice. The liver (shown below on the left) is your largest internal organ. It gives a final check to the blood coming from the digestive system – turning the nutrients into useful substances and filtering out any bad bits. It also produces bile, a liquid used to break down and digest fat.

LIVER? #1 **HEART?**

FIGHTING THE FAT

The bile produced by the liver is stored in the gall bladder. You need some fat in your diet because it stores energy for emergencies. So if the food arriving in the small intestine seems a bit fatty, the gall bladder squeezes out some bile. The bile breaks the fat down until it's ready to be absorbed by the body.

BLOOD CLEANING

It's really important for your body to get rid of the waste that it can't use. It sends all the solid waste from food down and out through your rectum. But all the chemical reactions going on in other parts of your body create even more waste. And that waste stays in your blood until it passes through another of your body's amazing systems – your kidneys.

Main vein

Main artery

Right kidney

Left kidney

Ureter

Bladder muscle

Bladder

Urethra

CLEANING SYSTEM

Your body always has about 5 litres (1.3 gallons) of blood flowing through it. The blood that leaves the digestive system is full of nutrients that are processed in other parts of the body. The chemical reactions that have processed the nutrients leave waste behind. So as the blood makes its way back to your heart, it passes through your two kidneys so it can be cleaned.

WATER WORKS

The kidneys filter your blood and the waste goes into a liquid, which is mostly water. This is called urine. The second part of the kidneys' job is to get rid of the urine, so the wastes don't remain in your body.

Cortex

Renal artery

Renal vein

Ureter

Medulla

FANTASTIC FILTERS

The real filtering work of the kidneys takes place inside the medulla, which look like shells. Each kidney has about a million nephrons (tiny blood vessels) inside the medulla to carry out this work.

KIDNEY MACHINE

A dialysis machine can help people whose kidneys aren't working well. The patient's blood passes through the machine, where it is filtered to remove harmful waste, extra salt and water. The blood then returns to the patient's body.

HEALTHY WEE

The kidneys control how much water is in your body. Yellow-golden urine is the sign of good health. Your urine looks clearer if your kidneys are getting rid of excess water. It becomes much darker if there isn't enough water in your system.

THE BIG THREE

CARBOHYDRATES
These break down into sugars that give you quick energy.

PROTEINS
The strength in your muscles is thanks to proteins.

FATS
These provide a 'storehouse' for energy.

THE POWER STATION

The digestive system – working all the way from your teeth to your stomach and intestines – does a great job of extracting all the nutrients that your body needs. You've also done your bit by making sure that your diet includes a good balance of carbohydrates, proteins and fats. So what happens to those nutrients once they've been sent off from the intestines?

GOOD NUTRITION

Your body needs a wide range of nutrients. The 'big three' group of nutrients are carbohydrates, proteins and fats. Some foods contain lots of one group. For example, a steak is high in protein and butter has lots of fat. But your overall diet should be a balance between them. A chicken sandwich is a good example of food that provides some of all three: the bread has carbohydrates, the chicken supplies protein and the butter supplies the fat.

During a match, tennis players often eat bananas. They are easy to digest and are high in carbohydrates, which the body uses to produce energy.

POWER UP

Proteins in food are broken down into pieces called amino acids. Your body then puts the amino acids back together to make different proteins that carry out special jobs. These new proteins help other chemical reactions, allow cells to communicate with each other, and even provide energy if there isn't enough carbohydrate or fat.

BREAKING THINGS DOWN

To release energy and keep you moving, your body uses chemical reactions to break down carbohydrates and fats. The bonds that hold some molecules together contain lots of energy, and breaking them apart releases that energy. This breaking down of bonds is called the catabolic process.

ENERGY

BUILDING THINGS UP

The opposite of the catabolic process is the anabolic process. Your body works with smaller molecules to produce larger ones. In this way it also builds new proteins.

ENERGY

AN ACTIVE YOU!

Together with a good, balanced diet, exercise helps to keep your body running smoothly. Taking some exercise, such as playing sport or going to a gym, also helps you to stay at a healthy weight.

Lungs
Breathing deeply helps the lungs stay strong

Muscles
Regular exercise strengthens muscles

Waistline
Energy needed for exercise burns some of the fat stored around your waist

Joints
Exercise keeps joints moving well

During your lifetime, you will eat about 27,000 kg (60,000 lb) of food – about the weight of six elephants!

BURNING CALORIES

A 'calorie' is a unit used to measure the energy stored in food and in your body. When you eat, the calories in food are turned into energy. If you eat more calories than your body needs for energy, those extra calories get stored as fat. Your body uses up calories just breathing, moving and thinking! But when you exercise, you need more energy, so your body burns up some of the calories stored as fat.

Heart
Exercise gives your heart a good workout – after all, it's a muscle too

ACTIVITY

There are 97 calories in 25 g (1 oz) of sugar. Look at the small print on a cola can, or chocolate bar, to see how much sugar it contains. Then, work out how many calories the sugar adds up to. Sugar should make up only 10 per cent of your daily calorie intake – which for adults is around 2,200 calories!

HOW MANY CALORIES?

There are 95 calories in 100 g (4 oz) of banana. Guess how many calories there are in 100 g (4 oz) of these foods. Answers are on the right.

Pork sausages

Banana

Chips

Broccoli

Strawberries

Apple

Celery

Roast chicken   Baked potato

DID YOU KNOW?

WHEN YOU BLUSH
THE LINING OF YOUR STOMACH ALSO BLUSHES

Your body produces a hormone called adrenaline when it needs to deal with stress. The adrenaline makes blood vessels widen so that more blood can flow through them. This increased flow causes certain areas of your body that contain lots of blood vessels – like your cheeks and stomach lining – to redden.

A TRADITIONAL DIET OF MEAT AND FISH KEEPS INUIT PEOPLE FREE OF MANY DISEASES

The Inuit people of the Arctic regions in the far north traditionally had little chance to eat fruit, vegetables or grains – foods that are considered essential for a balanced diet. In fact, the same vitamins and nutrients are plentiful in the types of oils and fats found in Arctic fish and meat.

AN ADULT WOULD HAVE TO RUN FOR 50 MINUTES TO BURN OFF THE CALORIES IN A SINGLE CAN OF COLA

Calories are a measure of energy. If you eat or drink more calories than you burn off through exercise, then you gain weight. You lose weight if you either eat less or exercise more. So an adult would need to exercise hard for nearly an hour to burn off the amount of energy – counted in calories – in one cola.

SALIVA
HAS LOTS OF DIFFERENT JOBS

Your salivary glands produce up to 1.5 l (53 fl oz) of this slippery liquid every day. And although the main job of saliva is to help begin the process of digestion, it performs other roles even when you're not eating. Saliva keeps your mouth moist, allowing you to swallow and speak, and it also helps to protect your teeth from harmful bacteria.

OPENING
YOUR MOUTH
TO EAT DOESN'T JUST LET THE
THE FOOD IN

As you open your mouth the air that flows in either raises or lowers the temperature of the food, to help it match your body temperature. Lots of what goes on when you digest food could be described as chemical reactions. And temperature plays a big part in making sure these reactions work. If one ingredient – such as very hot food or a very cold drink – is at the wrong temperature, then your digestive enzymes and acids can't work as well.

DOES CHEWING GUM

STAY INSIDE YOU FOR YEARS?

It's never a good idea to swallow gum – but the quick answer is no, gum doesn't stay inside for years. Chewing gum has four main ingredients – chemicals to give it taste, softeners, sweeteners and the gum base. Your body can digest the first three easily. The gum base is added so that you can chew it without digesting it. If you do swallow the gum, your digestive system recognizes it and passes it out like any other waste. But if you swallow too much gum in one go things could become blocked up and painful for a while 'down below'.

CAN YOU STILL SWALLOW AND DIGEST FOOD EVEN IF YOU ARE UPSIDE-DOWN?

Yes. And it's easy to understand why if you think of food travelling to your stomach from your mouth rather than down to your stomach. Your body doesn't need gravity to move the food along. Muscles in your gullet push the food along. As the food is pushed, the muscles behind it tighten and block it from going back to your mouth – even if you're upside-down.

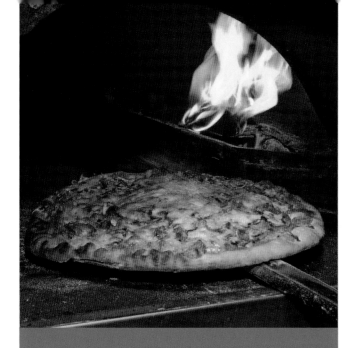

IS IT SAFE TO EXERCISE AFTER YOU'VE EATEN?

It can be, but doctors warn people not to exercise on a full – or an empty – stomach. Your digestive system needs blood to do its job, and it needs more blood after a big meal. The muscles you use to exercise also need blood, so you should be careful if you exercise hard after eating: you won't perform as well and you might get stomach cramps. But you shouldn't 'run on empty' either: those exercising muscles need the nutrients that are released by digestion. So make sure you eat before you exercise, but leave some time between the two.

WHAT MAKES YOUR STOMACH RUMBLE?

It rumbles because it's doing its job, except a little ahead of time! Your brain sends a signal to your digestive system when it senses food is on the way – maybe after you've bought a lovely cold ice cream or smelled some delicious pizza in the oven. The signals starts the muscles in your stomach and intestines tightening and loosening, just as they do when there's food to digest. But because they're empty, and there's no food to absorb the sounds, you hear rumbling.

SYSTEMS OF THE BODY

Skeletal system

The skeletal system supports and protects your body.

- Skull
- Sternum
- Ribs
- Humerus
- Backbone
- Radius
- Pelvis
- Ulna
- Femur
- Patella
- Fibula
- Tibia

Muscular system

The muscular system moves your body.

- Neck
- Shoulders
- Biceps
- Abdominals
- Quadriceps
- Calf muscles

Circulatory system

The circulatory system moves blood around your body.

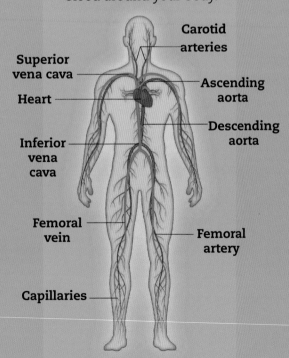

- Carotid arteries
- Superior vena cava
- Ascending aorta
- Heart
- Descending aorta
- Inferior vena cava
- Femoral vein
- Femoral artery
- Capillaries

Respiratory system

The respiratory system controls your breathing.

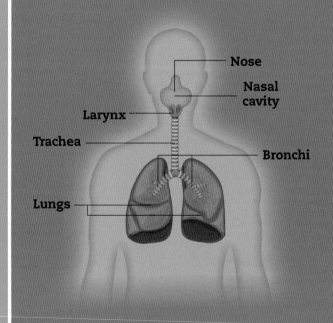

- Nose
- Nasal cavity
- Larynx
- Trachea
- Bronchi
- Lungs

This is your quick reference guide to the main systems of the body: skeletal, muscular, respiratory, circulatory, digestive, nervous, endocrine and lymphatic.

Digestive system

The digestive system takes food in and out of your body.

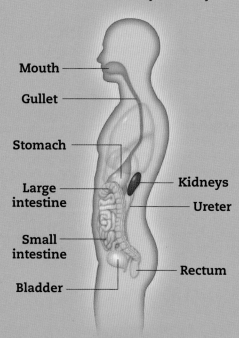

Mouth
Gullet
Stomach
Large intestine
Small intestine
Bladder
Kidneys
Ureter
Rectum

Nervous system

The nervous system carries messages around your body and controls everything you do.

Brain stem
Brain
Spinal cord
Radial nerve
Thoracic nerves
Sciatic nerve

Endocrine system

The endocrine system produces hormones and controls your growth and mood.

Hypothalamus
Thyroid gland
Liver
Kidney
Pituitary gland
Thymus
Stomach
Pancreas
Testes (male)
Ovaries (female)

Lymphatic system

The lymphatic system fights off germs and helps keep your body healthy.

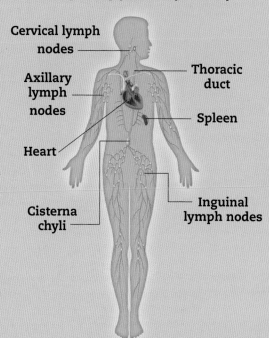

Cervical lymph nodes
Axillary lymph nodes
Heart
Cisterna chyli
Thoracic duct
Spleen
Inguinal lymph nodes

GLOSSARY

abdomen The area of your body just above and below your belly button. It contains your stomach, intestines and several other major organs.

amino acid An essential nutrient containing several chemical elements.

bacteria Tiny one-celled organisms.

bile A yellowish-brown fluid produced by the liver, stored in the gallbladder, which helps to break down fat.

calcium A chemical that is essential in the body for healthy bones and teeth.

calorie A unit for measuring the energy contained in food.

carbohydrate A type of sugar made by plants that the body uses to produce and store energy.

digestion The breakdown of food into substances that can be easily absorbed into the bloodstream.

enzyme A special protein that helps chemical reactions occur.

epiglottis The flap that folds down to prevent food going down the trachea.

fat A chemical substance that the body produces to store energy. It is stored in fat cells beneath the skin or surrounding organs.

gland An organ that regulates the release of hormones into the bloodstream.

gullet The foodpipe that connects the throat and the stomach.

hormone A chemical that helps to regulate processes such as reproduction and growth.

incisors The sharp teeth at the front of the mouth used to cut food into small pieces.

intestines The large and small intestines are the part of the digestive system where nutrients are released from the food into the bloodstream.

kidneys The organs that filter waste products from the blood.

liver A major organ in the digestive system which has many jobs including filtering the blood coming from the digestive system.

mineral A chemical substance, such as iron, which is important for health but which the body cannot produce.

molars The broad teeth at the back of the mouth that grind food.

molecule The smallest possible unit of a substance that still behaves like that substance. A molecule is made up of two or more atoms.

nutrient Any substance that the body needs for energy or growth.

organ A collection of cells that work together to perform a specific function.

peristalsis The contraction and relaxation of muscles that pushes substances such as food along a tube in the body.

protein One of the most important of all molecules in the body, protein is needed to strengthen and replace tissue in the body.

saliva The watery substance in your mouth that begins the process of digestion.

sphincter A ring of muscle that acts as a valve.

trachea (windpipe) The tube that connects the pharynx and larynx to the lungs.

urine The liquid waste filtered by your kidneys, taken to the bladder along the ureters.

vitamin A natural substance found in foods, but which the human body cannot produce, although it is necessary for good health.

zinc An essential mineral for the body found in foods such as meat, nuts and cereals.

FURTHER READING

Body Works by Anna Claybourne (QED Publishing, 2014)

Everything You Need to Know about the Human Body by Patricia MacNair (Kingfisher, 2011)

Horrible Science: Body Owner's Handbook by Nick Arnold (Scholastic Press, 2014)

How Your Body Works: Getting Energy by Philip Morgan (Franklin Watts, 2011)

Mind Webs: Human Body by Anna Claybourne (Wayland, 2014)

Project Science: Human Body by Sally Hewitt (Franklin Watts, 2012)

INDEX

BODYWORKS

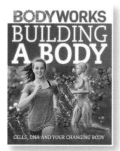

BUILDING A BODY
• Building a Body • All in the Mix • Body Builder • Back to Basics • Small Beginnings • Brand New You • Growing Up • You Are Unique • A Code for Life • All Part of the Family • Did You Know? • Frequently Asked Questions • Systems of the Body

DEFENSIVE ACTION
• Defensive Action • Germ Warfare • Rapid Response • Fighting Back • Lymphatic System • Temperature Control • Super Organs • Teamwork • Injury Time • Outside Help • Did You Know? • Frequently Asked Questions • Systems of the Body

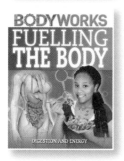

FUELLING THE BODY
• Fuelling the Body • Open Wide • Down the Hatch • Stomach Churning • Big and Small • A Balanced Diet • Helpful Allies • Blood Cleaning • The Power Station • An Active You! • Did You Know? • Frequently Asked Questions • Systems of the Body

LIFE SUPPORT
• Life Support • Have a Heart • Round and Round • Take Care of Your Heart • A Breath of Fresh Air • Speak Out! • Heart and Lung Facts • Testing Your Limits • Jack of All Trades • Get the Message? • Did You Know? • Frequently Asked Questions • Systems of the Body

READY FOR ACTION
• Ready for Action • The Skeleton Crew • The Hard Stuff • Meat on the Bones • Muscle Power • Working Non-Stop • Tying It All Together • Skin Deep • Tough as Nails • Spare Parts? • Did You Know? • Frequently Asked Questions • Systems of the Body

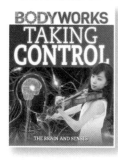

TAKING CONTROL
• Taking Control • The Brain Is Boss • What a Nerve! • Eye Spy • Hear, Hear! • Smells Good, Tastes Great • How Touching • Changing Your Mind • Behind the Scenes • Your Personal Computer? • Did You Know? • Frequently Asked Questions • Systems of the Body